DATE DUE

Even in Quiet Places

Even in Quiet Places

Poems by
William Stafford

Afterword by KIM STAFFORD

A James R. Hepworth Book

Confluence Press ◀▶ *Lewiston, Idaho*

IENTS

Some of these poems originally appeared in the following magazines: *Alembic, American Poetry in 1976, Cafe Solo, Calapooya Collage, Caliban, Chicago Review, Choice, Cimarron Review, Cow Creek Review, Crab Creek Review, Fine Madness, Inroads,* Inroads Press, *Interim, Kansas Quarterly, Licking River Review, New Letters, Nighthawk, Nightsun, Nimrod,* Northwoods Press, *Orbis, Oregon English, Panoply, Petroglyph, Plainsong, Poetry Kanto, Practices of the Wind, Publications of the Portland Audubon Society, Quarterly West, Red Dirt, Rhetoric Review, Sow's Ear, Spectrum, Sycamore Review, The Brown Journal of the Arts, The Chariton Review, The Christian Science Monitor, The Clockwatch Review, The Formalist, The Hampden-Sydney Review, The Kentucky Poetry Review, The Nation, The New Yorker, The New York Quarterly, The Northwest Magazine, The Northwest Review, The Oregonian, The Painted Circle, The Plum Review, The South Florida Review, The Southern Review, The Southwest Review, The Tampa Bay Review, The Western Humanities Review, University of Tampa Review, Utah Holiday, Willamette Journal of the Liberal Arts, Willow Springs, Writer's Forum.*

KIM STAFFORD and JIM HEPWORTH shaped this volume from four previous limited edition chapbooks: *Who Are You Really, Wanderer?* (Honeybrook Press, 1993); *Holding Onto the Grass* (Honeybrook Press, 1992); *History Is Loose Again* (Honeybrook Press, 1991); *The Methow River Poems* (Confluence Press, 1995).

Publication of this book is made possible, in part, by grants from the Idaho Commission on the Arts and the support of The Methow Institute Foundation and Lewis-Clark State College.

FIRST EDITION

Library of Congress Card Number: 95-71021
ISBN 1-881090-16-7 (paper) / 1-881090-19-1 (cloth)

Published by
Confluence Press
Lewis-Clark State College
Lewiston, Idaho 83501

Distributed by
National Book Network
4720-A Boston Way
Lanham, Maryland 20706

For You, Reader

Some Questions to Ask During Your Reading

*Have you a place where, when the world
ends, you want to be? Have you
a person who will be there when
you put out a hand? When the sky
weeps, whose fall will you weep?
Look steadily into the fire — what face
or sign do you see? If a fault is yours,
what forgiveness? Who will understand?*

— *William Stafford's original dedication to*
Holding Onto the Grass

Contents

HOLDING ONTO THE GRASS

HISTORY IS LOOSE AGAIN

THE METHOW RIVER POEMS

WHO ARE YOU REALLY, WANDERER?

Pages in the Language of Respect & Conciliation

1993

Another Language

Recently another language has grown up within the one others use. The new language has a special way: it avoids saying obvious things as if they are not so obvious; it never proclaims something that the kind of person being addressed is presumed to know already; it courteously gives credit to the needs but also to the dignity of the person addressed; it feels uncomfortable if it distorts the proportions of discourse—if under the pretense of being eloquent or fervent it dwells on self-serving statements.

This new language tolerates unconventional or "incorrect" talk or writing much more than it tolerates implicit discourtesy or dishonesty. The new language is the native tongue of those who grew up during that period when they found correctness used for deception, the years of official evasions and duplicity, Viet Nam and Watergate and on.

Speakers of the new language are seeking not just freedom of speech but freedom in speech—their own lives embodied in language.

Deep Light

From far a light, maybe a hill ranch
remote and unvisited, beams on the horizon
when we pass; then it is gone.
For the rest of our lives that far place
waits; it's an increment, one more
hollow that slips by out there, almost
a gift, an acquaintance taken away.

Still, beyond all ranches the deep
night waits, breathing when we breathe,
always ready to offer new light,
over and over, so long as we search
for something so faint most people
won't know, even when it is found.

Stray Moments

We used to ask—remember? We said,
". . . our daily bread." And it came.
Now we want more, and security too:
"You can't be too sure." And,
"Why should we trust?—Who says?"
And Old-Who doesn't speak any more.

They used to have Thunder talk, or
The Rivers, or Leaves, or Birds. It's all
"Cheep, cheep" now. It's a long time
since a cloud said anything helpful.
But last night a prophet was talking,
disguised as a clerk at the check-out stand:

"Gee, it's been a good day!"
And we talked for awhile and I felt
that I wasn't such a bad guy.
We stood there looking out at the evening.
And maybe what we said, in its way, was
Thanks for our daily bread.

History Display

Think of those generals at the wax museum,
and the women not present, but they're somewhere,
and all the histories those people escaped by being
in the one they were in. For an instant their wars
didn't happen and a heavy sweetness comes in the air,
like flowers without any cemetery, like my sister
holding her doll up to the window before
anyone told us about the rest of the world.

Those great people can stay where they are.
With love I erase our house and bend over our town
till the streets go dim and the courthouse begins
to dissolve quietly into its lilac hedge.
Some things are made out of rock, but some
don't have to be hard. They can hold it all still,
past and future at once, now, here.

Spirit of Place: Great Blue Heron

Out of their loneliness for each other
two reeds, or maybe two shadows, lurch
forward and become suddenly a life
lifted from dawn or the rain. It is
the wilderness come back again, a lagoon
with our city reflected in its eye.
We live by faith in such presences.

It is a test for us, that thin
but real, undulating figure that promises,
"If you keep faith I will exist
at the edge, where your vision joins
the sunlight and the rain: heads in the light,
feet that go down in the mud where the truth is."

All the Time

Evenings, after others go inside,
my glance quietly ascends through leaves,
through branches. The night wind sighs once
and bends over. Far beyond my glimpse of sky
those friends now gone begin their chorus.

There's a reason for whatever comes,
their song says. Released into light one star
appears, another, and those patterns affirm
where they have been waiting dissolved in blue
but holding their place inside of time.

Every evening this happens, an arch and promise
renewed. Nobody has to notice: a breath
crosses the lawn, or outside the window
a spirit roams, as mysterious as any wanderer
ever was. And it is only the night wind.

Being Young: Eleven

I dreamed I was dead—
it seemed I had assumed quiet, and
it turned out to be noisy. Only
belatedly did I realize that in fact
I had died. I couldn't get through
to the others to let them know
how I felt. A red police light
was revolving down the street.

When I woke in the morning and went into the yard,
locust trees were fluttering their feathery
leaves in a mild summer wind. I stood there
wanting to know, letting my attention go
everywhere, reaching out and being alive.

From down the street Sam trotted our way
kicking a can back and forth, one gutter to the other,
waving and leaning. His cap had the bill in back
so he could run fast. When he got to our house he
flipped the can in front of me, and we stood
together looking out over the fields.

We could work on our raft at the creek, or
put the roof on our cave. And there was
the hole in his backyard where we were digging
to China. My mother called out the door,
"Time for breakfast. What are you boys doing
today?" Over our heads the blue wind fluttered
the locust leaves. "Nothing," we said.

Back Home on Class Day

A tornado interrupted the speech about
what our future was. And enlarged
on the screen we saw foundations of our town
surrounded by ants holding them up with their hands.
Who would have thought fear when the river
came lovingly across our field? Lightning
revealed the sign that the bridge was down.

And it wasn't fair, that look Virginia
had—it twisted any home far away
into years of exile, and my life began to breathe
slower than the music was.
"Alone, alone," the bell said when school was out,
and every sunflower waved by the alley fence.

Facts

"Zurich is in the Alps." I learned
that, and had a fact. But I thought the Alps
were in South America. Then I learned
that's the Andes—the Alps are somewhere
else. And Zurich is famous, for something.

So I gave up fact and went to myth:
Zurich is the name of a tropical bird that
whets its bill on the ironwood tree in South America
singing about life and how good facts are.
The Alps are a people who raise reindeer, somewhere else.

Then it became important that the moon be
a close friend. I wanted the wind
always to make that same sound, sustaining
us through all the seasons, and always
around us—the night, and then the world.

Moons have changed many times by now,
and the wind has a voice more peremptory. Clear
nights have deepened all the way to the stars.
Zurich is famous and far from here,
and there isn't enough room for all the facts—

In this world.

Being Saved

We have all we need, some kind of sky and maybe
a piece of river. It doesn't take much more
if your ghost remembers the rest, how Aunt Flavia
called the cows in the evening, and there wasn't
anything coming down the road except a Ford
now and then, or a wagon with a lantern.

You could smell a little hay just to remind
the wind that sunlight would come back, and that
Heaven waited somewhere even if you couldn't see it.
I don't care now if the world goes backward—
we already had our show before the tornado came,
and somehow I feel in my hand all we ever held,
a ticket, a compass, a piece of iron,
our kind of pardon.

Playing the Game

Every rock says, "Your move," and then waits
till you do. After you turn away
it smirks—then suddenly still again
when almost caught. They'll crouch
till you die and then shout loud as a mountain.

You look at their little shoulders,
bent over but strong. Like them you
hunch against wind and that weight
pressing down—Time on its way somewhere,
using us all, people and rocks,
as a prop, as a wobbly crutch.

In a Country Churchyard

For Ruby N. Stafford

You little diggers and birds, things
that breathe, I have come to visit
your stillness here, to wander these woods
and find a grave. Will you help me?
The mourners have all long gone—and where
are the snowflake touches that grayed this board?

That snowflake that came, that day,
it clung the longest of all. "Winter," it said,
"I'm here." And the new letters, brave in the light,
shone on. Now, in today's dim light,
no one can read the name—too many
snowflakes, too many drops of rain.

But my fingers can still spell her legend here:
"I'm glad I came."

Big World, Little Man

"Some things it is wrong to think of,"
my mother said. "Don't think of them."
She was adjusting my scarf, sending me
off to school through the snow.

On the schoolground Orville would have me look up
and then he would hit me in the throat.
The flakes would look dark and come down
graceful and soft toward my eyes.

In the classroom after the bell
Miss Doherty always brought us in a circle
for reading, and I sat by Emily,
while outside the snow brushed past windows.

All of that comes meandering along,
even crowding into today—
falling in a long slant from the sky.
I stand here still, ready for then, for now.

Many things I do not think of.

Something You Should Know

They bring racing pigeons from everywhere
and set them loose at timed intervals from Little
America, out in Wyoming; every bird
circles high, sets a course, and banks
away toward its right place, the course for home.

I've watched them come, swift in the evening, wings
flashing in the last of the sun, diving steeply
down from the sky into some lone ranch in the junipers
lost to the world but centered for that pigeon's
life, the soul's direction sure. Like yours.

Like mine.

Over in Montana

Winter stops by for a visit each year.
Dead leaves cluster around. They know what is
coming. They listen to some silent song.

At a bend in the Missouri, up where
it's clear, teal and mallards lower
their wings and come gliding in.

A cottonwood grove gets ready. Limbs
reach out. They touch and shiver.
These nights are going to get cold.

Stars will sharpen and glitter. They make
their strange signs in a rigid pattern
above hollow trees and burrows and houses—

The great story weaves closer and closer, millions of
touches, wide spaces lying out in the open,
huddles of brush and grass, all the little lives.

A Story I Have to Tell You

They made a wolf out of sheet iron
and planted it where it inherited rust
in all weathers on a cliff in the wilderness.

I found it there and heard a strange howl
from its hollow mouth when the wind blew
reveille, as a gift from The North for us.

Is it only air when a sound comes?
Maybe The Great Meaning begins
to stir within the commonest things.

Maybe I shouldn't have listened. Maybe
that howl was only for me. Forgive me,
friends—but it was iron, it was cold.

And I was there.

Farrier Talk

They said a mule with the right mother
could be tractable, enduring, an admirable steed.

They said racehorses may wear aluminum shoes
or even titanium; and some shoes are glued on.

You have to be ready, they said, you have to
think like the horse.

There is a world organization of farriers,
with meetings all over, like in Morocco.

If you live in easy country and don't
work your horses hard, they can go barefoot.

In the face of danger a horse does
what it is best at, it runs.

A Farewell, Age Ten

While its owner looks away I touch the rabbit.
Its long soft ears fold back under my hand.
Miles of yellow wheat bend; their leaves
rustle away and wait for the sun and wind.

This day belongs to my uncle. This is his farm.
We have stopped on our journey; when my father says to
we will go on, leaving this paradise, leaving
the family place. We have my father's job.

Like him, I will be strong all of my life.
We are men. If we squint our eyes in the sun
we will see far. I'm ready. It's good, this resolve.
But I will never pet the rabbit again.

Sometimes

When they criticize you how do you
hold your wings? I hold mine out
and down, descend a little, then more.
Cool air comes. Nobody cares how low
I descend, and the way my eyes close
makes me disappear. They have their sky again.

So thin a life I have, scribbling dust
when I turn, trailing as if to follow
something inside the earth, something beyond
this place. If I accept what comes,
another sky is there. My serious face
bends to the ground, the dust, the lowered wings.

A Glimpse, Age Five

Our mother was pretty sure. She held her
dark little face near us, and her lips
went into a firm line. "The devil waits
right under your feet, and when you lie
or do wrong, poof!—you're gone."
"Just like a bubble," she said. We looked down.

Hell extended everywhere, we knew that. Bad children
burned there. For some reason the devil
gave us his personal attention. He
helped us be good—no special treatment.
Peg and I looked at each other. Her red hair
framed a round, chubby face, and her eyes
looked for reassurance or guidance from mine.

Outside in the front yard we worked on
our playhouse and ground two old bricks together
to make topping for mud pies. We didn't
talk about what Mother said. Under our feet
the devil watchfully followed wherever we went.

Old Prof

He wants to go north. His life has become
observations about what others
have said, and he wants to go north. Up there
far enough you might hear the world, not
what people say. Maybe a road will discover
those reasons that the real travelers had.

Sometimes he looks at the map above
Moose Jaw and thinks about silence up there.
Late at night he opens an atlas
and follows the last road, then hovers
at a ghost town, letting the snow have whatever
it wants. Silence extends farther
and farther, till dawn finds the same page
and nothing has moved all night, except
that his head has bowed and rested on his arms.

Rousing to get started, he has his coffee.
He sets forth toward class. Instead of the north,
he lets an aspirin whisper through his veins.

Poetry

Its door opens near. It's a shrine
by the road, it's a flower in the parking lot
of The Pentagon, it says, "Look around,
listen. Feel the air." It interrupts
international telephone lines with a tune.
When traffic lines jam, it gets out
and dances on the bridge. If great people
get distracted by fame they forget
this essential kind of breathing
and they die inside their gold shell.
When caravans cross deserts
it is the secret treasure hidden under the jewels.

Sometimes commanders take us over, and they
try to impose their whole universe,
how to succeed by daily calculation:
I can't eat that bread.

In The Book

A hand appears.
It writes on the wall.
Just a hand moving in the air
and writing on the wall.

A voice comes and says the words,
"You have been weighed,
you have been judged,
and have failed."

The hand disappears, the voice
fades away into silence.
And a spirit stirs and fills
the room, all space, all things.

All this in The Book
asks, "What have you done wrong?"
But The Spirit says,
"Come to me, who need comfort."

And the hand, the wall, the voice
are gone, but The Spirit is everywhere.
The story ends inside the book,
but outside, wherever you are—

It goes on.

Holding onto the Grass

1992

That Day

Have the phone ready;
then right where time touches the edge
have the phone ring and it be —
well, it could be only Yusif or Arabella
telling when they'll arrive.

But maybe that ringing goes on
even when you lift the phone.
Maybe the sound wanders away
outdoors and along the street
into the country.

And it won't stop. It takes you far
toward the trees where they wait
for new light, for quiet. They won't answer.
Then mushrooms will speak:
the soft answer you need.

Then you can come back, breathing.

Report to Someone

We think we're all there is, then the big light,
and a call comes and everyone understands.
All right, we're lonely:—trees never need us, and
wind in its wandering visits us then goes away.
And we can't see it but we think there's a light inside
everything. Even at night it wants out and pushes
quietly, insistently on the wall with its tiny hands.

In the silence that comes flooding down from the mountains
a shapeless lament begins to press toward sound.
It can wait: it gains by every day
of being unrecognized. Without moving
it explores a way to be ready, and when
pieces of time break off it follows them,
alive in their being and unknown but true.

With Apologies All Around

Now it seems that I am not sad enough. Some
terrible thing has happened and I only
shift my eyes to the moon coming up
or how the water catches the light.

And besides, my eyes keep following
a sentence that someone is saying. My head
accepts and it nods and hurries to say,
"And another thing . . . ."

Meanwhile that big sadness hangs on
back there. What business do I have
with my easy agreeableness: "You're right,"
"Sure enough, it's that way," "Please tell me more."

So I'll try to be sad. For all my wanderings,
my thoughtless delights, I'm sorry.

One of the Stories

A square of color on Rayl's Hill
was a place where we often walked—
there under a new-killed Indian brave
pioneers buried a child.

Once the tough grass that strangles flowers
is broken, you can't hide what's buried—
a burst of color will mark that square
for years on the open prairie.

Out there in the sun an outlaw man
driven from his tribe killed a girl
because he couldn't stand her tears
when he frightened her there on the hill

The settlers found and surrounded the man
and the father killed him in rage.
All around the prairie lay.
And the settlers were afraid.

Fearful, at night, the parents dug,
and beneath the Indian brave
to protect their own they hid the girl
from hate that could tear up a grave.

My father showed us that special square
with many a flower twined
for the double burial, one above one,
where death was used as a blind.

"Bandits may kill but be innocent,
and children may die but sin:
no one but God sees all the way down,"
our parents told us then.

And for years our family tended that place
with fear, with wonder, with prayers,
where God had sprung the prairie flowers
from whosever grave it was.

For Robert I. Stafford

Caterpillars measure you, our mother
said, for any suit the years may bring,
and such a very careful measuring
that when the butterflies become their other
life the cloth they weave by colored wing
will stretch—they'll find a fit for anything
the sun can touch. I bend and reach our father
where he lies far back there—again, again.
Remember the catalpa trees? Our neighbor
who dug the hole to China one afternoon
with us? No flights of butterflies will ever
smother home, how soft those coats were, Brother.

Grace Abounding

Air crowds into my cell so considerately
that the jailer forgets this kind of gift
and thinks I'm alone. Such unnoticed largesse
smuggled by day floods over me,
or here come grass, turns in the road,
a branch or stone significantly strewn
where it wouldn't need to be.

Such times abide for a pilgrim, who all through
a story or a life may live in grace, that blind
benevolent side of even the fiercest world,
and might—even in oppression or neglect—
not care if it's friend or enemy, caught up
in a dance where no one feels need or fear:

I'm saved in this big world by unforseen
friends, or times when only a glance
from a passenger beside me, or just the tired
branch of a willow inclining toward earth,
may teach me how to join earth and sky.

After a Sleazy Show

No warning was posted there in the theater
where ordinary people began to encounter
evil, no skull and crossbones on the slick
packages of dope in the story, no surgeon general's
announcement that the language of drugs
has a long-term influence on ears
that become dulled and then unable to separate
good speech from the jabber of crime.

When the lights came on the listeners looked at each other
and thought they were the same. That slow filming,
equal over all eyes, kept the audience calm
while their lives were annulled. A new ice age
crept closer. Outside on the street bright ads
promoted the next show and pictures of a life
with zing and popularity. Everyone hurried toward
the corner, new attractions, louder promises.

My NEA Poem

A blank place on the page,
like this here "———,"
means, oh it means,
you know, but not said.

And it is better when you come to these
"———"s again
to leave blank places.

But some people
get a grant
and want to show
artistic freedom;

So all they say is,
"———,"
"———,"
and "———."

You Forget

Often in high school some quick sun-arrow
glanced, usually in late afternoon,
and all the lessons turned gold. Your desk
drifted from others but felt firm
and spoke its promise to you: "Forever."

In later years what others thought
wouldn't count. Armored with your need,
you treasured those afternoons that brightened as
they arrived. And they meant all of your life,
even the parts nobody else knew:—

Those bells in the heart, that dulcimer,
and the days walking beside you, their glances
level, equal—permanent moments that suddenly
come back now, tunneling to redeem those days,
those years now lost, that were true.

Learning to Adjust

At the store they gave me the wrong
package, but I took it home and decided
to live with it. Why complain? Why
upset the clerk or the manager? Besides
this package might be more than
I deserve. Look—it has a whole tangle
of ribbons around it and many greetings
and slogans: "Be happy." "Return to sender."
"Who is Terza McDonald?" "For you,
Pig Head." Your life already
has enough puzzles, and returning anything
just complicates the plot. A gift
is a gift. Just what you always wanted.

Men

After a war come the memorials—
tanks, cutlasses, men with cigars.
If women are there they adore
and are saved, shielding their children.

For a long time people rehearse
just how it happened, and you have to learn
how important all that armament was—
and it really could happen again.

So the women and children can wait, whatever
their importance might have been, and they
come to stand around the memorials
and listen some more and be grateful, and smell the cigars.

Then, if your side has won, they explain
how the system works and if you just let it
go on it will prevail everywhere.
And they establish foundations and give
some of the money back.

Distractions

Think about Gypsies—
like smoke in the evening they cross a border.
They don't believe in it, and they say if God
doesn't care nobody cares. In the morning
their wagons are gone, carrying their stories
away. They like the sound of a wheel
and have given up owning a place. They roll
beyond old newspapers and broken glass and
start a new campfire. Sometimes, going up
a steep hill, they get off and walk forward
and whisper the oldest secret in the world
into the ears of their horses.

Pretend You Live in a Room

Play like you had a war. Hardly anyone
got killed except thousands of the enemy,
and many go around starving, holding
their hands out in pictures, begging.

Their houses, even the concrete and iron,
they've disappeared. These people
now live camped in the open. Overhead
stars keep telling their old, old story.

You have this world. You wander the earth.
You can't live in a room.

From the Ink on This Page

An old barn could hold out its dreams. Day
would bend over and surround it with slices of sunlight.
An artist would climb over the mountains
for that certain shadow, a splinter that comes
exploring when chance wakes up in the loft.

You could move little people around and then
slam a mountain over their farms, or tease
them till they charge foolishly down into the sea.
Their heroes will posture a bit before drowning,
and one might actually survive and come back, for awhile.

You can put those pieces away in their box.
Pictures on the outside will remind everyone
of other lives, of tigers that wait, claws
ready to pounce, or of how some people
hold out their hands forever in a golden rain.

Getting Here

"Utah restores your soul." Window
was talking. Aisle leaned over to see:
"Therapeutic all the way."
It was easy to know—
they were talking to Middle, me.

Window fixed on my eyes:
"Did your parents love you?"
"Did my parents love me—*me?*
They didn't beat me, though,
and maybe that passes for love."

Aisle was not amused:
"You need the Moab country."
And Window quickly agreed:
"When air comes by at dawn you can
smell that Indian medicine—
it's Utah air you need."

Then Aisle nodded across
and both of them looked at me.
Did my parents love me? Me?
If you're in the middle, you know,
all you can see is wing—

Well, maybe a piece of sky
while the miles of therapy pass
and you crane to look now and then.
But then if you're in Utah
maybe that's all you need.

Up a Side Canyon

They have trained the water to talk, and it prattles
along a stone trough contoured by the house,
following its instinct, unafraid of rock
or of anything but rest. It never decides,
"This is the place," but tells its long
history far up the canyon, a shivering life
we forgot, that we need more than a city,
more than any new vision. An old silence
waits beyond water, or road, or trail.

Inside the house they have draped the pelt
of a black bear, its glittering eyes on the past;
and they spread the soft fur of an arctic
wolf that came by a strange path
all the way from Russia to this hidden room
where at night the water talks and the bear
looks at the wolf, like a tawny dream
of Siberia. People go silent:
there isn't any canyon deep enough to hide,
only a sky and a faith and a wilderness.

East of Broken Top

Sunset reaches out, earth rolls free
yet clings hard to what passes.
Light pours unstinting, though darkness
cuts the horizon and leaps for the sky.
Beyond, in a shadow vast as the world,
a silent upland springs blue where it stands
morning and evening. Its own being,
it never changes while the light plays over it.

We could go there and live, have a place,
a shoulder of earth, watch days
find their way onward in their serious march
where nothing happens but each one is gone.
Some people build cities and live there;
they hurry and shout. We lie on the earth;
to keep from falling into the stars we reach
as wide as we can and hold onto the grass.

In the All-Verbs Navaho World

"The Navaho world is made of verbs."

Left-alone grow-things wait, rustle-grass, click-
trunk, whisper-leaf. You go-people miss the hold-still
dawn, arch-over sky, the jump-everywhere glances.
This woman world, fall-into eyes, reaches out her
makes-tremble beauty, trolls with her body, her
move-everything walk. All-now, our breathe-always
life extends, extends. Change. Change your live-here,
tick-tock hours. Catch all the flit-flit birds,
eat the offer-food, ride over clop-clop land,
our great holds-us-up, wear-a-crown kingdom.

Malheur Before Dawn

An owl sound wandered along the road with me.
I didn't hear it—I breathed it into my ears.

Little ones at first, the stars retired, leaving
polished little circles on the sky for awhile.

Then the sun began to shout from below the horizon.
Throngs of birds campaigned, their music a tent of sound.

From across a pond, out of the mist,
one drake made a V and said its name.

Some vast animal of air began to rouse
from the reeds and lean outward.

Frogs discovered their national anthem again.
I didn't know a ditch could hold so much joy.

So magic a time it was that I was both brave and afraid.
Some day like this might save the world.

For Our Party Last Night

It was necessary at the time that the sun
go down — veiled, orange, perfect—
just a touch on the far hills, and that a half moon
hang at a silver height. It was all necessary.
Then where we sat we discussed the news
about art, should it be free. Should our country
support even what shocked some reluctant
people who had to pay. By then in the dusk
fireflies came out. The far hills, mounds of trees,
moved nearer. A lawyer said, "Let the artist paint
but the state needn't pay at all." An artist
said, "But without a living what does freedom mean?"
And by then the stars had spread in a great
arc. At our table where a candle burned
our faces gathered on that little center of light,
while the dark leaned in, large and cool and necessary.

Knowing Where You Are

One time a clock said midnight,
or else it said noon—we were in a cave
and couldn't be sure. And it was on an island—
at least, I think it was.

Is there any way in a cave like that
to know if it is midnight?
It's the same old number, no matter
what you say, so what difference does it make?

And if an island moves is it the same
island but in a new place?
If I moved away I wouldn't change
more than I had to.

So if anyone asks, I always
just say, "Noon."

Some Names

Some only whispers, they have faded.

Some like big rocks, you have to go around them.

A few are hard to say,
    your voice doesn't like them.

One sounds thin, like a lost bird,
    or some little person's jacket crumpled
    by the road, or a lost sweater.

And one can't quite get said, even when
    you are bowed down alone. It is
    wandering somewhere in the mountains.

Survival Course

This is the grip, like this:
both hands. You can close
your eyes if you like. When I say,
"Now," it's time. Don't wait
or it's all over. But not
too soon, either—just right.
Don't worry. Let's go.
Both hands.

HISTORY IS LOOSE AGAIN

1991

How You Know

Everyone first hears the news as a child,
surrounded by money-changers and pharisees;
then later, from gray trees on a winter day,
amid all the twittering, one flash of sound
escapes along a creek—some fanatic among
the warblers broken loose like a missionary
sent out to the hinterland, and though the doors
that open along the creek stay closed for the cold,
and the gray people in their habitats don't look out,
you—a homeless walker stabbed by that bird cry—
stop mid-stride because out of a thicket
that little tongue turns history loose again, and holy
days asleep in the calendar wake up and chime.

Listening to the Tide

Tomorrows ago the world spun
a different way, we are told. One pearl morning
arrived so still that the ocean stopped.
And then there followed a single smooth wave,

A single smooth wave evenly
spread in gray light horizonward. Thinking
of that, and of how nothing
can hold back for long a wave that comes,

And the wave that comes after that, beginning
tomorrows to here—we're afraid. Listen—
one distant sound made all the rest,
they say—one tremendous explosion,

One tremendous explosion that could come
again, and a wave, and a wave, and a wave.

Good Thought

Bent over a ship in a bottle, on an island
in a lake on an island, farther within
than the sea in the world we sailed around—
we find the grommets are laced, sail furled, paint
renewed; and our lives lean out and come back
escaping time and place, more sudden
than light. We think—"Any old summer!—
who needs a companion?" And we're ready to go.

In the Library

You are reading a book, and think you know
the end, but others can't wait—they crowd
on the shelves, breathing. You stop and look around.
It is the best time: evening is coming,
a bronze haze has captured the sun,
lights down the street come on.

You turn a page carefully. Over your shoulder
another day has watched what you do
and written it down in that book
you can't read till all the pages are done.

A Note Slid Under the Door

Some people don't know this:

A sound lower than silence
begins out of the night that waits
lower than silence, and the voice
descends finer than dust or moonlight
where people awake listen
beyond the dark, finer than
dust and the mistake called life.

In that breath beyond silence
people awake hear this:

"It is the same if you die
or if the world is destroyed—
the world is here because
people found it, a faint
line low in the sky, then
an island, or mainland, then
the place where you live.
Afterward, after you are gone,
the world won't be there any more."

Some people don't know this.

La Bohème

The music said sorrow. It said Mimi was dead,
that the stars don't know we exist. It said
no one can ever tell it all.
The fire at Hellgate burned in a barrel
for street sweepers, for cold workers
at dawn; and the flute—buried under
horns and kettledrums—prattled of its long
infatuation with sunlight (that one
star that cares). It is not the people,
it is not winter, or whatever surrounds us, that counts:
what the music sought was there.
It had survived all through the silence.
After the stars, it would still be there.

Even in the Desert

You know how willow is. Well, there was
this girl evolution stopped at:
the way a tree accepts the wind
when it roves the country this girl would bend.

When the wind found her one day, she
followed where it went, like a snowflake
in love, ravishing. You know that lake
over by China Peak? When last seen
the two of them, girl and wind—and one
other, Death—were dancing toward the waves.

The way wind is, and how it moves,
and the long promises, the centuries of trust,
had easily captured evolution's girl.
Her soul still sleeps in this beautiful dust.

The Bent-Over Ones

Some trees look down when
they walk, certain willows
you know, all the way from
Louisiana to Alaska without
looking up. They studied
centuries of buffalo grass
toward Dakota. I have
traveled among foreign
trees. Some of them kneel
when they approach mountains.
Like them I have learned quite
a bit about the ground.

Bristlecone

A sky so blue it hurts frames
all else, and in silence this oldest thing
alive clenches on edges it found
long ago and began to grow.

Almost freed of life, this tree
weathers nobly, yielding back nine thousand
growth rings to the bracing air that
hums with sunlight even while it freezes.

A raven shadow touches us;
we get stronger, just by being
here, almost freed by the sun.

The Way Trees Began

Before the trees came, when only grass
and stones lived in the world, one day
Wanderer heaped up a mound of mold
from dead stems and breathed on it.

You could look for miles then; sunlight
flooded the ground, and waves in the air
combined with billowing purples of grass
when you stared over open hills.

That mound stayed still in the sun, and at night
it quivered a little in the grass-rippled wind,
but Wanderer forgot and went on over miles
where shoulders of rock hunched from the ground.

You know what began, after warm and cold,
after trembles and sighs that gradually
awakened:—a tiny furled-up leaf
spread out in the wind and waved like a hand.

Time was slow back then, a thick
slow golden syrup that flowed
over everything. It was good to the leaf
and to others that came, waved, and were gone.

Till now—trees everywhere. Wanderer
touches them in the spring, and they remember
how lonely it was. One little leaf at a time
comes out and begins all over again.

Watching Sandhill Cranes

Spirits among us have departed—friends,
relatives, neighbors: we can't find them.
If we search and call, the sky merely waits.
Then some day here come the cranes
planing in from cloud or mist—sharp,
lonely spears, awkwardly graceful.
They reach for the land; they stalk
the ploughed fields, not letting us near,
not quite our own, not quite the world's.

People go by and pull over to watch. They
peer and point and wonder. It is because
these travelers, these far wanderers,
plane down and yearn in a reaching
flight. They extend our life,
piercing through space to reappear
quietly, undeniably, where we are.

Weeds in a Vacant Lot

We know that it's our fault, these effluent suburbs,
the great population spill that we are, and our trash
that thickets of scrub will try to contain.
Return, wilderness; what we held
for awhile we will give back. Singly
as we depart we will bequeath our temporary
vainglorious, posturing conquests—back to
the pampas grass, the forgiving vines
that embrace auto carcasses, refrigerators and
their spilled treasure, the bulldozed
garbage of our civilization.

We know that it's us, the stink
in the sky, the machine that can't stop:
"We are coming; we will bury you."
But we leave space where we can—any place left vacant
fills with volunteers bivouacking till their time
arrives. The great soft hope of the milkweed
explodes, and the wind carries its parachutes
and salvation wherever development hesitates
or allows, even for a season, an opening
for our ultimate friends, these quiet
relentless, healing adversaries.

By the Chapel

We stood around for awhile and John said,
"This is where I begin to feel the sky. If you wait
for it, after someone is gone, or even in a cave,
or at night, it comes near and leans on you.
Afterward, any touch will connect far away."

That's what John said while we waited there.

And it's true if you lean carefully and listen you hear
someone who used to wait with you, and you don't care
if the sky comes or if anything tries to comfort.
So I couldn't argue with John. My shoulder
ached for his bowing so long without any help.

And a voice in my ear did sound good, and near.

A Presence

A shadow dawns inside my shadow,
and a voice my voice contains; a hand has
curled like a glove on my strengthened hand—

A charge—a surge in color and sound,
that world in a heightened curve—has come,
force in the season, an enhancement of being.

I hear an interval that isn't a storm
calling: that voice commands the legions
of snow, and all my allegiance follows.

I swing into knowledge and fall, all
the way into tomorrow, away from friends,
thin voices that fade in this new dawning.

January's Child

My life arrived in winter, wrapped
in fur. Ears heard the darkness, hands
explored a wall. All night a wind reminded
"This is the world."

Silent spectators, my parents and I
observed this great drama
and lived it in our bone houses:
"Life and the cold."

Those monuments cling to me—those years,
towns, houses where we lived,
and now these, my children,
and myself grown old.

Freedom of Expression

My feet wait there listening, and when
they dislike what happens they begin
to press on the floor. They know when
it is time to walk out on a program. Pretty soon
they are moving, and as the program fades
you can hear the sound of my feet on gravel.

If you have feet with standards, you too
may be reminded—you need not
accept what's given. You gamblers,
pimps, braggarts, oppressive people:—
"Not here," my feet are saying, "no thanks;
let me out of this." And I'm gone.

Coming to Know

A balloon ascends on that path it finds in the air
fated for it before the world began,
and my eyes following find what they have to find
because they are here and wide and helplessly mine.
A face on the side of that balloon not yet alive
leers forth at what it intends, later,
to know. My face hides, afraid of knowing
too soon that revolution in the expanse of the sky:—

My father's face dawning in that of his son,
alert, fierce enough to survive, but soft
enough to learn in time how balloons will rise,
inevitable, stronger than steel, firm on their path
exactly where Now becomes itself, printed
on a face in the sky, or here like this in a man.

Someone You Don't Know

Walking into a hall, not pressing, never
pressing, I stop just inside the door. If the
place is cold, I'll be cold. Whatever happens,
I'll yield. Attracted somewhere, I go.

A person carrying a package walks toward
me; I step aside. *Remember—never touch one.*
Sometimes I overhear talk ("How can I make him
believe . . . ?" "I am going to give her something
to be sorry for"), and the temptation to speak
almost overwhelms me, but I wait. It does
no good to tell them anything.

All the slow evening I drift from group
to group, listening, never catching anyone's
eye, never quite taking my place. Gradually
the hall empties, lights go out, the hollow
silence I love grows wider and wider. Long
after everyone is gone, I stand in a small
pool of moonlight from a high window, making
no sound, making no shadow.

It Returns At Times

Where is that grief I had, the one
that followed me along every street?
It waited outside a door, beginning its patient
chant: "Far from where you are, hidden by dark
or light, the terrible crimes go on, too many
to stop or lighten, overwhelming sometimes."

Among shirts in their closet with their empty
sleeves—among coats that embrace only air—
my old grief hides. Doors close; lights click;
footsteps count off into silence; and there
my old grief bows in its corner again.
It lives on in its quiet, at home in the dark,
tugging a sleeve sometimes for a word,
for a gesture, for a warm coat.

Twelve

Early leaves are tender. They shiver
in the cold wind. Once in the spring
I had a friend.

Pure chance, it was, our meeting
on the way home — school was out.
Linda was her name.

Remember the sky leans back,
some people you meet? And it's blue out there?
This was like that.

Linda was taken away. It's the story
of my whole life — that first shiver
of spring, of love.

Cottonwood

By June or July the river flows lazily
shallow and clear among sandbar islands,
and I wade it, zigzag, exploring upstream
where tracks of raccoon, possum, and waterbirds
form a design to be read. Over it all
from millions of saplings that stretch on north,
deep and immense, there arches the odor of cottonwood.

That certain tang in the air, maybe it wrapped
and protected Crazy Horse; it hovered over his blood
when they killed him. It freshened the laundry spread out
in groves where mothers hung washing for wagon trains.
It hovered The West, reminding in the new church,
or jail or tavern, that a great sweep of air waited
beyond, outside, in long curves of the river.

Every breeze brings that pungent but delicate smell.
Embracing the day, I carry it homeward
on hands and clothes, not knowing how sacred
these days: twelve years old, June, July, cottonwood.

Looking Out in the Morning: Carson City

I.

In Nevada we ordinary people carry our money
and throw it into machines for the rich to collect
and haul away in trucks with bars on the windows
or in their long dark, mysterious limousines.

II.

Will anything we ever did or will do last as long
as a flint arrowhead in the hills?
But what difference is time?—a flower on a yucca,
a plume of mist in the morning air, a theory—
these all flicker by even as boulders do
when they last only a few million years.

III.

But the universe turned over once and stayed,
when I looked up and my child across all
that ever happened or would happen was staring
everything that there is into my eyes.

Time Goes By

On a corner you meet a face. It follows you,
and at night even after your eyes
are closed the face is there waiting.

Or, sometimes a tune begins in your head
and it won't stop. No matter how
important the moment, the tune goes on.

When I was in school, a girl at a picnic
sang a song. It was autumn
and her face in the firelight overcame shadows.

Listen—there is a sound beyond
every sound, and there is a face almost
glimpsed, like a friend's, when shadows move.

How It Can Be

People can drift farther apart. They can
move away and try never to be heard from.
The colors they wore will gradually relate
to other people. Places will change after
a time and there will be fewer and fewer reminders.
It will be different. Snow will cover old paths.

Woodsmoke will continue to tell its old stories,
and I'm sorry about that, but when autumn comes
we can travel wherever we want and either
work or move on, even across the ocean,
and not pay any attention to the stars
or to certain songs if we hear them.

Sometimes a dog like our old one will run by;
roosters will crow like those every morning for so long,
but—you know—it will change. New trees
will grow. Beacons on high places everywhere
in the world will go on blinking over and over.

Bad Dreams

1.

You are wounded, but at first you think
it's a badge. Dying, you hear applause—
your death rattle. Afterward your home
place becomes a freeway. Every tire
slaps its design on your face—again, again.

2.

You gradually turn into yourself; any mask
looks the same. It begins to have
that "me too" look. You turn away
and count ten, turn back and stand proud:
for an instant it could be all right—someone else.
Then you sag into you.

3.

As you go down the street you begin
to unwind, like a raveling sweater. A car
snags a thread and whirls away part
of you. A person shakes hands and your hand
trails off when he leaves. You are a bobbin
unspinning, and the last part left is one hand
holding the pen writing this.

4.

You're gone.

Influential Writers

Some of them write too loud.

Some write the mauve poem
    over and over.

In our time a whole tribe have
    campaigned with noisy boots on—
    they look swashbuckling but
    all the syllables finally run and hide.

Their swagger makes them feel good,
    but mobilizes opposition.

Listen—after a torrent begins even big rocks
    have to get out of the way,
    but at the top of the divide you can change
    Mississippi to Columbia with one finger,
    and I did.

But I didn't want the Pacific this big.

For the Chair of Any Committee I'm On

If you value my opinion, please be
   sure I understand the question.

I am not deaf or blind, but I do not
   hear or see all things equally well.

Experience is always coming along:
   sometimes I change.

I do not demand a right to prevail, or
   even to be heard: on some things, if
   you want my opinion you must ask.

In regard to budgets and wages: in all
   my lifetime I have been unable to rid
   myself of a tendency to favor equality.

A Child of Luck

Once I feel bad, it takes chocolate
or maybe a trumpet gone silver
in the air to redeem the time,
but always till now some coin
flips, and the chance is mine.

Remember when Mother died?—
the birds wouldn't stop calling
their names, and a redbird sang
autumn to flame. My ears
opened; they drank that song.

Every street in our town, every farm
on the way to forever, gladdens
my life. Listen—how loud
all conspires: I hear
the days coming, that chocolate sound.

Browser

Is there another book that was
hidden throughout the terrible years?

Back of history, leading afar
when the armies marched
on the heads of the people,
was there a way too fine
for the blundering stumbling multitude?

Along old shelves, peering
at neglected volumes passed over
by others, I grope in the shadow.

Some day, back of upright
books I will encounter that line
winding secretly through time.
And the truth will plummet into my eyes.

The Methow River Poems

1995

Being a Person

Be a person here. Stand by the river, invoke
the owls. Invoke winter, then spring.
Let any season that wants to come here make its own
call. After that sound goes away, wait.

A slow bubble rises through the earth
and begins to include sky, stars, all space,
even the outracing, expanding thought.
Come back and hear the little sound again.

Suddenly this dream you are having matches
everyone's dream, and the result is the world.
If a different call came there wouldn't be any
world, or you, or the river, or the owls calling.

How you stand here is important. How you
listen for the next things to happen. How you breathe.

Silver Star

To be a mountain you have to climb alone
and accept all that rain and snow. You have to look
far away when evening comes. If a forest
grows, you care; you stand there leaning against
the wind, waiting for someone with faith enough
to ask you to move. Great stones will tumble
against each other and gouge your sides. A storm
will live somewhere in your canyons hoarding its lightning.

If you are lucky, people will give you a dignified
name and bring crowds to admire how sturdy you are,
how long you can hold still for the camera. And some time,
they say, if you last long enough you will hear God;
a voice will roll down from the sky and all your patience
will be rewarded. The whole world will hear it: "Well done."

Where We Are

Fog in the morning here
will make some of the world far away
and the near only a hint. But rain
will feel its blind progress along the valley,
tapping to convert one boulder at a time
into a glistening fact. Daylight will love what came.
Whatever fits will be welcome, whatever
steps back in the fog will disappear
and hardly exist. You hear the river
saying a prayer for all that's gone.

Far over the valley there is an island
for everything left; and our own island
will drift there too, unless we hold on,
unless we tap like this: "Friend,
are you there? Will you touch when
you pass, like the rain?"

Ask Me

Some time when the river is ice ask me
mistakes I have made. Ask me whether
what I have done is my life. Others
have come in their slow way into
my thought, and some have tried to help
or to hurt: ask me what difference
their strongest love or hate has made.

I will listen to what you say.
You and I can turn and look
at the silent river and wait. We know
the current is there, hidden; and there
are comings and goings from miles away
that hold the stillness exactly before us.
What the river says, that is what I say.

Is This Feeling About the West Real?

All their lives out here some people know
they live in a hemisphere beyond what Columbus discovered.
These people look out and wonder: Is it magic? Is it
the oceans of air off the Pacific? You can't
walk through it without wrapping a new
piece of time around you, a readiness for a meadowlark,
that brinkmanship a dawn can carry for lucky people
all through the day.

But if you don't get it, this bonus, you can
go home full of denial, and live out your years.
Great waves can pass unnoticed outside your door;
stars can pound silently on the roof; your teakettle
and cosy life inside can deny everything outside—
whole mountain ranges, history, the holocaust,
sainthood, Crazy Horse.

Listen—something else hovers out here, not
color, not outlines or depth when air
relieves distance by hazing far mountains,
but some total feeling or other world
almost coming forward, like when a bell sounds
and then leaves a whole countryside waiting.

From the Wild People

Time used to live here.
It likes to find places like this
and then leave so quietly
that nothing wakes up.

Whenever a rock finds what it likes
it hardly ever changes. Oh, rain
can persuade it, or maybe a river
out looking around. But that's the exception.

They say there was a time when
rocks liked to dance. You can see
where that happened—great piles
of old partners that got tired of each other.

Now and then one stirs when nobody
is looking; then it stops and looks away
humming a little tune. In the mountains
you can see those nonchalant rocks.

Some of them should have stopped sooner—
they're haggard old wrecks, friendless,
and often just slumped around
wherever they fell.

Time for Serenity, Anyone?

I like to live in the sound of water,
in the feel of mountain air. A sharp
reminder hits me: this world still is alive;
it stretches out there shivering toward its own
creation, and I'm part of it. Even my breathing
enters into the elaborate give-and-take,
this bowing to sun and moon, day or night,
winter, summer, storm, still—this tranquil
chaos that seems to be going somewhere.
This wilderness with a great peacefulness in it.
This motionless turmoil, this everything dance.

A Valley Like This

Sometimes you look at an empty valley like this,
and suddenly the air is filled with snow.
That is the way the whole world happened—
there was nothing, and then. . .

But maybe some time you will look out and even
the mountains are gone, the world become nothing
again. What can a person do to help
bring back the world?

We have to watch it and then look at each other.
Together we hold it close and carefully
save it, like a bubble that can disappear
if we don't watch out.

Please think about this as you go on. Breathe on the world.
Hold out your hands to it. When mornings and evenings
roll along, watch how they open and close, how they
invite you to the long party that your life is.

You Can't See It, But

Under the earth a great river has found
its own life. A torrent of stone
surfaces and congeals. We share that aftermath
in its stony garden. Stilled, Earth's history
poses for study, levels of shale. Roots
delve for messages to turn into flowers,
messages the dirt hides all winter.

Past those earth signals we are led blundering,
beyond fainter signals too fine for our
sight. Our hearts race only for oxygen;
meanwhile the story of Heaven plays itself
inside rooms we can't see.

From This Lookout Point

The cast here, in order of disappearance, were
dinosaurs, sabre tooths, many birds, pioneers,
Shoshones, Wolverines, Wolves, Grizzlies.
For some reason they don't come around much any more.

Also certain people have gone away—saints,
explorers. They didn't want to disturb the air.
All those tracks in river sand—gone.
And their fires, the charcoal—all washed away.

So sometimes I choose a cloud and let it
cross the sky floating me off there too.
Or a bird unravels its song and carries me
as it flies deeper and deeper into the woods.

Such times, laments are not necessary. You could
wait here all winter and the mountains would
just stand there. They wouldn't say anything. Why
should they care? Someday everything will be gone.

Hey, let's hurry down and forget this.
It gets cold here.

I'm Any Old Tree

Look at me. My family are gone. I am old and alone.
I built my house on the sand. My limbs are tired,
want to rest on the ground. How can a life extend?
Today, left here, I stand bowed like this
and remember: little birds, crows, years
when the sun studied this land for lives like mine
to admire. Look at me—if my part of the world
ever hears that wind again that came, my shuddering
roots will die. And you—around this place
miles of wilderness flow out soft and alive.
They flow for us all. They give and return in the wind.
And the little birds trill. I'll endure. And you? And you?

You Reading This: Stop

Don't just stay tangled up in your life.
Out there in some river or cave where you
could have been, some absolute, lonely
dawn may arrive and begin the story
that means what everything is about.

So don't just look, either:
let your whole self drift like a breath and learn
its way down through the trees. Let that fine
waterfall-smoke filter its gone, magnified presence
all though the forest. Stand here till all that
you were can wander away and come back slowly,
carrying a strange new flavor into your life.
Feel it? That's what we mean. So don't just
read this—rub your thought over it.

Now you can go on.

Emily, This Place, and You

She got out of the car here one day,
and it was snowing a little. She could see
little glimpses of those mountains, and away down
there by the river the curtain of snow would
shift, and those deep secret places looked
all the more mysterious. It was quiet, you know.

Her life seemed quiet, too. There had been troubles,
sure—everyone has some. But now, looking out there,
she felt easy, at home in the world—maybe like
a casual snowflake. And some people loved her.
She would remember that. And remember this place.

As you will, wherever you go after this day,
just a stop by the road, and a glimpse of someone's life,
and your own, too, how you can look out any time,
just being part of things, getting used to being a person,
taking it easy, you know.

It's Like This

It's like this—time opens
a door here. You find yourselves alone. That's when
in this big room that sound begins again.
To get away you have to come here and hide
as if you belong here, looking casually away.
You see, it's that sound. It starts almost like silence,
then an excited, repressed voice. Then
louder, faster. You have to look around,
get away, get out of here. You can't
bear to listen for long, it's too intense.
But you have to find if it still goes on,
after these years. You see, there is something
beyond music. If you get there, you look around
quickly before the air breaks up into those
pieces of glass, the hail with claws in it.
People who find that sound shake from sympathy,
and what they held off for long can leap upon them
and put the ultimate blade into their hearts,
you see, and then twist, like this.

"Nobody cares..."

Nobody cares if you stop here. You can
look for hours, gaze out over the forest.
And the sounds are yours too—take away
how the wind either whispers or begins to
get ambitious. If you let the silence of
afternoon pool around you, that serenity
may last a long time, and you can take it
along. A slant sun, mornings or evenings,
will deepen the canyons, and you can carry away
that purple, how it gathers and fades for hours.
This whole world is yours, you know. You can
breathe it and think about it and dream it after this
wherever you go. It's all right. Nobody cares.

Pretty Good Day

Before day around here
light begins. Then there won't
be many stars. The creek tells its own story
while day listens for what comes next. All stories
add up to where you are now.

Certain loyalties dictate where the river goes.
Of them all, the greatest is to the sun, but evasion
feels pretty good too. And this river
likes evasion.

Water likes to sing. If you leave it alone,
even in quiet places, it'll talk a little
to itself about old days it has known
and the songs it composed.

Days around here don't want any more
history to happen. They linger in the evening
and let go after a long quiet
purple consideration.

There are stories here for church windows, and
the one about the lazy beaver, the one where a face
begins to belong to somebody else, and that
classic: "The Last Day and Superfact."

Real People

Trees are afraid of storms. Even big ones
will do anything when the wind blows—
they'll bow, they'll spend their branches.

In the tropics, imprisoned by vines, one race of giants
has stood around for centuries teased by lightning
and snakes. Their hearts have grown hard
as iron, and limbs have writhed out a jungle story.

A whole forest in Siberia fell at the knees of
an unknown emperor so terrible no one ever
said his name, and those trees never got up again.

If you go hiking up in the mountains
you find miles of stumps where trees have
run away, panicked by the sound of a saw.

There is one tribe that has trudged far north
to wait with little round shoulders for the cruel snow.
Sometimes one raven wings by asking where justice is,
and low along streams there—the abject willows.
They're poor. They never ask for anything.

The Whole Thing

Does it make any differences what you see
every day? And hear? And smell? And feel?
And know is over the horizon? Who shares it
with you? Whether it is permanent or fleeting?

If the horizon is a straight line, that's
the world you are seeing. But a tree or
a mountain will cut off part of the world.
So, in some places the world is very still,
and permanent. These trees and boulders, cliffs,
vistas without any plan—they are waiting.
These presences don't notice you, but they have
endless patience and courtesy.
And over the years the calls of meadowlarks
in the morning have rinsed off these upland
parts of the world. I think we should keep
some of this, in case God comes back
to see what we did with it.

What Gets Away

Little things hide. Sometimes they
scuttle away like dry leaves in a sudden
wind. Tidepools are full of these
panicky creatures, and rock slides
have jittery populations hidden from the world
and even from each other.

Herodotus tells about the shyest
animal there is. It's the one even
Alexander the Great and his whole
conquering army had never seen, and people
—no matter how hard they try—
will never see.

William Stafford's Quiet Places: An Afterword

by Kim Stafford

When my father died, in August of 1993, it was a shock to many, despite his age of 79. He seemed an immortal to some, an enduring part of the literary landscape, especially where that landscape borders on friendship. He left thousands of poems to his readers. He left to me, as his literary executor, a myriad of decisions: what to do with the last poems, unfinished projects, and projects never to be finished. We have established an archive for much of that legacy, and people send us additional materials, and there are still decisions to make and projects to carry out, in family consultation, but this particular collection lies clearly in the category of projects to be finished by kindred spirits now. How you breathe your way through these lines by William Stafford depends on how you thirst for certain quiet places in your own life. I am talking about the quiet place that stands for a departed friend, or the sweet trance inside a book you love, or some old tree, some riverbend that summons for you the quiet of your own spirit. My father had them, and you have them, these seclusions of place and thought. This book is about the kinship we share because we know these things.

It has been my privilege to work closely with the publisher of Confluence Press, Jim Hepworth, to create this book. We see it as a companion to *My Name Is William Tell* (Confluence Press, 1992), which brought together poems from five chapbooks printed by Donnell Hunter of Honeybrook Press: *Stories and Storms and Strangers* (1984), *Brother Wind* (1986), *You and Some Other Characters* (1987), *Annie-Over*

(1988), *Fin, Feather, Fur* (1989); and from *How to Hold Your Arms When It Rains* (Confluence Press 1990). In parallel fashion *Even in Quiet Places* collects three subsequent chapbooks from Honeybrook Press and concludes with a cluster of poems from a late project, the Methow River poems. When Confluence Press decided to publish *My Name Is William Tell*, my father asked Donnell Hunter to select poems from the four chapbooks and to rearrange these poems in a new order. With *Even in Quiet Places*, we kept to the order of the individual chapbooks as William Stafford knew them, gathered here in reverse chronological order: *Who Are You Really, Wanderer?* (1993); *Holding onto the Grass* (1992); and *History Is Loose Again* (1991). We decided to begin this book with *Wanderer* (1993) because it opens with the manifesto, "Another Language," and because we believe the subsequent poems in that chapbook have a pronounced authorial presence that orients what follows. We also decided to end this collection with the Methow River poems, a set of utterances William Stafford contributed to two enterprising forest rangers when they asked him for what they called poetry road signs. He submitted some twenty poems, and seven were chosen. These seven have since been etched and mounted on signs along the North Cascades highway in Washington (and also published in a chapbook, *The Methow River Poems*, Confluence Press, 1995). Of these seven, six are unpublished in book form, and are included here in this book's closing section (the seventh, "Ask Me," originally appeared in *The New Yorker* and then in *Stories That Could Be True*, Harper & Row, 1977). This book thus gathers William Stafford's most recent work conceived for small press publication and regional expression.

With that in mind, I want to turn now to a consideration of my father's poetic practice, particularly as exemplified in the Methow poems, for I believe the Methow poems display in the extreme a habit of mind that not only characterizes this book as a whole but my father's life work.

The last poems in this book, then, my father submitted to the Methow River sign project, with his customary prolific generosity.

Some poems seem quickly made, hit or miss, almost random things, but with deft nuggets of insight. I think of Edward Weston's last photograph, that image of scattered rocks and sand at Point Lobos, a kind of reduction of universal spin to the elements of its original making. Unlike his classic images under the spell of the group called *f/* 64, with their pure look at compact forms, Weston's last image shows a widening, a letting go.

I think also here of Joan Miro's late paintings from Majorca, the large, open canvases with a few bold strokes. I think of "Traveling Through the Dark," pushing that one small life away, letting it go back into the river of change. I think of my father's sly poem from the 1970s, "Things I Learned Last Week," which smuggles into a sequence of observations this one strange prophecy:

> If I ever die, I'd like it to be
> in the evening. That way, I'll have
> all the dark to go with me, and no one
> will see how I begin to hobble along.

William Stafford wrote poems of release all his life, but the Methow poems seem particularly relaxed. What do we make of a line like, "How you stand here is important"? The line hardly says anything, asserts nothing in particular, turns in place clear as water or air. And yet, I remember how much this clarity can mean. I remember many, many times in the forty-four years I knew my father when he expressed a wisdom that felt the opposite of control. I remember a mountain road at midnight, when we huddled around the car by flashlight to change a tire. There was a distant sound of motorcycles, big ones, a swarm approaching. This was the territory of California, in a time that felt dangerous. We were far from any help. Might desperados not take our party, kill the men, and pluck the women away? I was ready to crouch, desperate, with the tire iron clenched in my hand. As the gang swung around the curve toward us, I looked at my father, and I was amazed. He was standing with the most pronounced nonchalance I had ever seen, a kind of studied slouch. His baggy pants helped, and the way he leaned back onto his left heel, face turned up. It was the quiet, the insistent, the unmistakable posture of a pacifist: *Nothing is going to happen. You can do as you will. You will not draw me into violence.* Headlights caught us. The gang slowed, stared, then swung on past, their departing black fringe and chrome leaving us quiet in the dark.

Yes, how you stand is important, "How you listen for the next things to happen." Readers of William Stafford know he can be fervent, trenchant, tough:

> I have joined the ambulance or the patrol
> screaming toward some drama, the kind of end
> that Berky must have some day, if she isn't dead.
> ("Thinking for Berky")

But in these poems, "in the language of respect and conciliation," this book enters the power, the equilibrium of old ways, even in quiet places.

The poems my father contributed to the Methow project form a distinctive conclusion to this new book, and, if it is not too grand to say so, an unusual enrichment to the literary history of the American landscape. Thoreau carried through life the ambition to write a book completely outside. He didn't do it. My father carried an ambition, as I read his work, to return to the landscape as spirit in a state of conciliation: "My self shall be the plain, / wise as winter is gray, / pure as cold posts go / pacing toward what I know." That was his announcement in an early poem ("The Farm on the Great Plains"), and that is his achievement in this project at the end of his life. He *is* the series of seven posts pacing along that tall highway they have to close in winter. After the ice eases its grip, you can stand by the road along the Methow River in the Cascade mountains of Washington state, in a very quiet place, and read, "I like to live in the sound of water. . . ." William Stafford speaks of the place, at the place. The experience of reading these poems in place closes the circle of William Stafford's approach to poetry, where the poem makes no greater claim than the sound of the water itself, a small and immense utterance. And when he dies, his words invite us back into that sound, the resonance of the book of the world.

The phrase "even in quiet places," from the poem he called "Pretty Good Day," identifies a prevailing spirit in this book, particularly in the Methow River poems, intended as they are to accompany a traveler in the landscape. Speaking in the voice of tree and river, an intrinsic elder of the land, these poems ask a traveler, "Who are you, really?" There is here a quiet kind of reversal of the grand tradition, of Yeats with his "Horseman, pass by!" William Stafford's epitaph is every poem he wrote that says the opposite: Wanderer, reside. Reside in the local, in the truth of this place "so faint most people / won't know, even when it is found."

The consistent witness of William Stafford's life and work appears in many local particulars in this collection. The subtitle of the first section, "Pages in the Language of Respect & Conciliation," recalls his life-long position as a pacifist and fifty-year member of the Fellowship of Reconciliation. Many poems testify to the clarity of landscape and language that accompanied his Kansas boyhood, where "Still, beyond all the ranches the deep / night waits." His sense of identity with endangered places and people—the original and enduring claim of the local—appears everywhere.

At the very end of his life, my father had typed a form letter to alert the world to his long-deferred true retirement. His plan was apparently to send a copy of this letter in response to invitations to read, to teach, or otherwise engage the public. As far as I know, he never got around to using this letter prior to his death in August of 1993, but the language he composed as a farewell can stand us well here:

> . . . I leave my place to the young, the talented, and the ambitious. And I willingly accept life on the shelf.

Did he, willingly? Yes, there are poems here of farewell. But are we survivors classed among the young and the ambitious? He taught us too well the limits of ambition, of "success" in any terms but the engagement of full personal witness in a dangerous but strangely sustaining world: "Speakers of the new language are seeking not just freedom of speech but freedom in speech—their own lives embodied in language." Against these words, the bill of rights becomes a weak and passive document: a pacifist enacting truth must go beyond it.

I miss many things about my father—his humor, his calm, his perennial youth: "How you listen for the next things to happen." One thing I miss is the way he was so eager to listen and savor what others brought to him. One of his poems has his father say to him, "Your job is to find out what the world is trying to be." Genesis is the responsibility of everyone. This was the heart of his teaching and writing, his "starting with little things." There is a certain dimension that seems to identify the 'subjects' of William Stafford's poems, a dimension that is at once very small, very ordinary, hidden, and at the same time immense, fundamental, universal. A willow tree's anguish of offering, a meadowlark's fiddling call, a young girl's brief look—there is no limit to the importance of these gestures the world makes: "Come back and hear the little sound again." If there is one longing I feel, it is to share these beginnings, these little things, in his company, and savor their full magnitude in the attention he would give. But if his teaching is true, we can do this alone. If he could travel so far outside himself—the distances spanned by poems here like "Men" or "Even in the Desert"—so can anyone.

What do these poems invite us to do? William Stafford's witness did not stop on the page. I remember that time a woman in the audience said aloud during a William Stafford reading, "Why, these poems are so simple, I could have written them myself." And my father replied to her, "But you didn't." She looked up at him, and he said, "but you could write your own." Without some version of writing our own—poems, lives, quiet place—we will be like those commanders who "die inside their gold shell." But by writing, by creating new life out of local materials, we may inherit the world.

In the poem here called "Spirit of Place: Great Blue Heron," I remember how my father connected the worlds that others divide. We were in Washington, D.C., for a big gathering at the Library of Congress. The greats of contemporary poetry were to be there, and my father would enter the grand and public swirl. But first, he had an assignment from home, a request from Mayor Bud Clark of Portland, Oregon, to write a poem about the Heron which had just been adopted as the city's official bird. After dressing for the national event, my father loosened his tie and lay down on the motel bed, and there wrote this poem. All things join "out of their loneliness for each other": wilderness and city, far Oregon and the Capitol, tall head in the light and deep reach in the mud. By his deft attention, his pen stroke joins us close.

I still have the feeling he is ready to converge any time, to get together, to trade recent discoveries and inventions. He must be there, at the edge of the crowd with his camera, or just up the canyon, where he has rambled alone. He'll come by, and we'll talk. When stories of a certain size, or ideas with a certain kind of torque, when tentative apprehensions come to mind, he is a listening place. I remember a bookstore in disarray, where the shrewd proprietor tested my sincerity with a few sharp questions, then showed me how to slide away the outer row of ragged paperbacks on each shelf to find the first edition poetry books hidden in the row behind. That is the kind of story my father would savor. It would probably turn up, transformed, in his daily writings very soon.

My father would savor that story. I can't tell it to him now. What does this mean? He taught me—taught us simply to notice such things. I look up from my writing today to see a hummingbird hovering before my face, and I know my father would share my readiness to experience the visitor: "bright little savior." Or this: yesterday I heard a story about a couple in their nineties, my wife's ancestors, joining a wagon train of the 1830s on a whim in their buggy, crossing the continent in the company of more ambitious and serious people, feasting on the provisions others carried. I want to tell my father this. I want to tell him how the old man would play his fiddle in the evenings at one edge of the circled wagons out on the prairie, while his wife led a prayer meeting at the opposing edge. Somehow that circle of prayer and fiddletune, that little event on the wide plain, feels like a William Stafford poem. He could have written it. But he did not. So I can write my own. And I do. It is evening. I join him in this delight, here on the mountain where I tell him softly, softly in this quiet place of each other, and the story, and you.

Kim Stafford
August 6, 1995

FOR YOU

It is a secret still, but already your tree
is chosen. It has entered a forest for miles
and hides deep in a valley by a river.
No one else finds it; the sun passes over
not noticing. But even while you are reading
you happen to think of that tree, no matter where
sentences go, talking about other things.
The author tries to be casual, to turn
from the secret. But you know exactly what is out there.

You set forth alone.

—— *William Stafford's original dedication to*
            Who Are You Really, Wanderer?

Index of Titles

About the Author

William Stafford was born in Hutchinson, Kansas, in 1914, and studied at the University of Kansas and the University of Iowa, where he received his doctorate. At intervals during his schooling, he worked as a laborer in sugar beet fields, on construction jobs, and in an oil refinery. He married Dorothy Frantz in 1944. During World War II William Stafford worked in alternative service as a conscientious objector for four years, in Forest Service and Soil Conservation camps, going on to serve with The Brethren Service Commission and Church World Service.

He taught high school in California and in colleges and universities in California, Alaska, Indiana, Kansas, Washington, and Ohio. He joined the faculty of Lewis and Clark College in Portland, Oregon, in 1948 and taught there as a professor of English until his retirement from full-time academic teaching. As a poet, he won not only the National Book Award for his volume *Traveling Through the Dark* (1962) but also the Shelley Memorial Award and the Award in Literature of the American Academy and Institute of Arts and Letters. He served as Consultant in Poetry for the Library of Congress (1970-71) and on the Literature Comission of the National Council for Teachers of English. The U.S. Information Service sent him to lecture in such places as Egypt, India, Pakistan, Iran, Nepal, Bangladesh, Singapore, and Thailand. In poetry he published 51 books by 35 "small" presses during his lifetime and another eight collections with HarperCollins in New York. The most recent of the Harper books is a selected poems edited by Robert Bly entitled *The Darkness Around Us Is Deep* (1993).

In August of 1993, William Stafford died at his home in Lake Oswego, Oregon, where he and Dorothy had raised their four children, Bret, Kim, Kit, and Barbara.

Colophon

Even in Quiet Places was set on the Macintosh by Caroline Hagen in Monotype Baskerville. The display and figures are Goudy Italian Old Style. This book is printed by Cushing-Malloy on acid-free paper. The cloth edition is limited to 1500 copies.